Past Providence

Bob Watts

David Robert Books

Published by David Robert Books
P.O. Box 541106
Cincinnati, OH 45254-1106

Typeset in Garamond by WordTech Communications LLC, Cincinnati, OH

ISBN: 1932339760
LCCN: 2004110024

Poetry Editor: Kevin Walzer
Business Editor: Lori Jareo

Visit us on the web at www.davidrobertbooks.com

Past Providence

Acknowledgments

Grateful acknowledgment is made to the following journals, in which these poems were first published:

New York Quarterly: "Eureka Springs," "On Beauty"
The Paris Review: "The Light at Hinkson Creek," "A Poly-Grecian Urn: Wal-Mart, Easter Weekend, 1998"
Pembroke: "Cicadas," "Driving Home," "Last Harvest," "Reading the Leaves"
Poetry: "The Idea of Landscape"
storySouth: "Lot"
Southeast Review: "The Fall Apart," "Late Night Hymn," "Penelope Redecorates," "Soracte," "Taking the Cake"
Southern Poetry Review: "Child of Age"

Sections of "Cemetery Orchard: A Ghost Story" were published, sometimes in substantially different form, in *The Edge City Review, Southern Poetry Review,* and *Voices: The Art and Science of Psychotherapy.*

I wish to thank the following people, without whom this book could not exist, and to whom these poems are dedicated: "The Idea of Landscape" to Sherod Santos; "Leaving the Garden" to Lynne McMahon; "Child of Age" to Gerald Barrax; "My Grandfather Waits for Sleep" to Joanie Mackowski; and "For the Dead One" and "Seed Time" to the memory of Ralph Edward Watts, 1922-2002.

For my parents,
Ralph and Mary Watts,

and for Stephanie,
always, my love.

Contents

Late Night Hymn

Jesus, who else would call this late,
  murmuring 3 AM's
low promises of paradise,
  as if a whispered "Come,"

could still yank me erect, or drop
  me trembling to my knees,
slack-jawed and stupid with desire.
  Give it a rest; give me

a rest. Nights now, I only rise
  to piss, and don't stay up
past twelve for anything, too tired
  for talk or drink or love.

So tell me why I sit awake
  to watch this shuck of moon
decline against the dark, or why
  I take the wind's low moan

brushing dry pine across the brick
  as your late call, the grind
of rusted hinges on a door
  I thought I'd closed for good.

I.

The Idea of Landscape

There will be no trees there,
no split-barked sycamore
ascending, spirit and flesh
caught in rough metaphor,

no flare of sweet gum leaves
as the refining fire
for light stropped keen
on steep October air,

no branch of shumard oak
in leafless underline
to the silhouettes of crows
against the sky,

nothing higher than ourselves
not made by us to throw
the shadow of a veil
between the barest earth

and unencumbered blue
scrubbed to emptiness
by the long wind through
the hair unnumbered on our heads.

The Light at Hinkson Creek

One final fall of sun slips past the ridge
behind my shoulder, coats the upper limbs
of a creek-side sycamore in gold too rich
for February, then settles on a stream
dead still, the clumps of foam scattered across
the water hung like fruit on mirrored trees.
The light seems somehow brighter brought to rest,
entangled in the far bank's canopy—
the earthbound branches leafless, mottled gray
and silver-white, the rough bark's loosening curls
inverted in immaculate relief,
and shimmering at my fingertips, so close
I have to reach for it, the twice-bent gleam
that passes in the swirl my reaching makes.

A Poly-Grecian Urn: Wal-Mart, Easter Weekend, 1998

I.

Half-ravished by the first light touch of sun
  on winter-languid skin, and air's slow stir—
ardent, close—across bare limbs, we've come
  for potting soil, for silver-bladed trowels,
for the brightest daubs of color we can bear
away, pre-blossomed in black plastic flats
 of vinca, dianthus, pansies. Months too late
 to raise the tulips' complex pulse, we praise
   instead the ready-made, until it takes
     the squat shape of this bastard child of Keats.

II.

Maybe we've come to this—all that remains
  the pointless simulacrum of a choice:
white or green, it's plastic either way,
  machine-stamped in the hollow shape of loss.
Or is this too much to make of a cardboard nest
 of two-part urns, bowls and bases packed
  as snug as bullets in a magazine,
  arranged for sale in monochromatic stacks,
the scraps of half-truth and cheap beauty rent
  to pieces by this dying century?

III.

The two of us are young enough to dream
 we'll make it out alive, somehow escape
the burden of our genes and history
 to start again, unstained. From the rotting corpse
of a lion he'd killed, Samson took honey, ate,
 and found it sweet, but then slew thirty men
because of it. Like him, we crave the taste
 of something drawn from death, but can't be sure
 if fingers drip with syrup or with gore.
 Or both. Nothing we touch is innocent.

IV.

A block away, pale-bellied leaves, wind-wheeled,
 invoke the storm, but just beyond the gate,
my neighbor's yard's a fuchsia-tinted peace
 of statuary petals, as if the air
were stunned to silence, stillness, by the brute
 beauty of a redbud's blooms. I go inside,
 come back to limbs still shaking, stripped of leaf
and blossom, and sidewalks scrawled in a green hand
just clear enough for me to read the truth,
 that beauty couldn't even save itself.

V.

I fill the urn with pansies, purple, white,
 and pink, but nothing lives past the first rain,
when water pools around a sodden welt
 of storm-pressed flowers. The planter doesn't drain;
its certitude drowns everything I put
 in it. I dump the slop of store-bought loam
 and flaccid stems, then cut thin slits to bleed
 the water out, and try again, a need
to keep something alive, if nothing more
than these doomed blossoms in a plastic pot.

Soracte

Look at Soracte, its bright weight
of snow. Look at the trees. They can't
bear more, bent close to breaking. The steep
        streams stop, ice-bound.

So turn away, build up the fire,
uncork the '98 Merlot
and let it breathe. The world will take
        care of itself.

Time turning to tomorrow will
silence the storm; the white-peaked waves
will still, the sea-wind beating
        through the cypresses

and bare-limbed ash will lie, the branches
tremble to rest. Let them. And spend
each new day's windfall while it's green.
        Night calls you now

to lend your whisper to love's swelling
chorus—a giggle caught beneath
a quilt, a rising breath, a soft
        cry from a dark

backseat, a boy, his fingers fumbling
with his belt, a girl, lifting her hips
the barest inch to let him—help him?—
        ease her jeans down.

Sunrise Service

Behind a ridge-long silhouette
        of spring-leafed oaks,
the Easter sun elaborates
        the horizon's simple stroke

of black into an upward swirl,
        and I'm afraid
that *this* is the morning He'll return;
        but it's just the sun that breaks

the sky today, nothing but light
        that sweeps across
our road, the Caudle's doublewide,
        their tall, tin-roofed garage,

and a dozen rows of tombstones set
        in family lines.
Some dawn, these graves will split and let
        the dead ascend to join

Christ in the clouds, the quick called last,
        ripped in surprise
from cars and kitchens, shower stalls
        or morning exercise.

Not all will die, but all will change,
        and they can't wait,
these graveyard singers joined in praise
        of a sure and certain faith

of life past flesh. I should be ardent
        for that day to come,
but in my mind I see the parting,
        not the coming home:

the newborn torn from its mother's reach
               in awful innocence;
the trailing clouds of tangled sheets
          behind two lovers clenched

in a sacrament of sweat-slick breasts,
             clasped hands, backs arched—
the earthly falling from the blessed,
         moaning a late aubade

to the pull of God, of gravity,
             of letting go.
Some dawn, but not this one, serene,
         graves still as weathered stone,

the empty sky an indifferent tint
             of fading blue.
Up from the grave he arose, we sing—
         our voices, visible

in the cold, rise from us, note by note
             become the air,
and vanish as I watch them go,
         caught up without a prayer.

Autumn Clerestory

What promise rustles to be read
    within the pointillistic light
of this wind-fretted vault of dead
    and dying leaves? That solace lies

    beyond the candor of bare limbs?
Of time's sure pull against our grasp
    on this green world? Or an afterlife
as luminous as saint-stained glass,

an ardor bright when flesh has passed?
    That's what we hope: that death reveals
some buried brilliance long possessed,
    releases us to catch the deep

        umber passion of the oak,
        the maple's flare of letting go.

Past Providence

My Saturn's shadow streaks downhill,
  a block-long blur, weightless,
and nimble as the spill
       of leaves it races

past Providence and up Broadway.
  Due east, where they become
mere loveliness, drained
       of danger, storm

clouds grind together, shape themselves
  into the perfect arcs
of hills, familiar curves
       distant and dark.

Or I shape them, faux mountains made
  of air and my desire
to feel earth fall away,
       to stand wind-scoured,

clean. Almost, I believe my road
  curls upslope to those summits
and cuts a path through stone
       obscured by mist

but as concrete as the facades
  that frame this easy street
of restaurants, student bars—
       juice, coffee, beer—

storefront displays of hiking gear,
  and the sidewalk parade
of ersatz poverty
       our privilege wears.

Columbia's low ridge can't lift
  its crest above the sway
of still ascendant limbs,
        the shallow waves

of poplar, oak and sweet gum peaked
  with early color, flakes
of gold, vermilion streaks.
        I want to break

the careful boundaries of my life,
  be swept away in fear
and beauty, bear the fire
        these bright leaves feed

their moment to, and yet not be
  consumed, as if that force—
God's word? Something more deeply
        interfused?

A momentary elegance
  composed of cloud and leaf,
the play of sun against
        old brick, the soft,

almost imagined shimmer of
  the air above the road,
the shoppers set to cross,
        the final notes

of a Billie Holiday CD
  lingering in my mind
after the song has ceased,
        and how this blends,

the whole of it, with what I feel
 and think of it? Can all
this resonate and leave
            without result?

The things of our world lead to love,
 if we give them the chance,
move from us as we move,
            half-seen, changing

like the car-struck shadow that skips
 through autumn's oblique light
and leads me up the slope
            to where home waits,

consolation in its earthly graces,
 pleasures of bed and cup,
redemption with a face
            and human touch.

Cicadas

If we become too full to be
  contained by flesh finally as frail
  as these chitin husks that cling to curls
of elm and maple bark, or weave

vague rows across the white-washed walls
  of our garage—so loose they lose
direction, become no rows at all,
  scattered like cars left driverless

and bumper-stickered in the wake
  of raptured saints—if we too seek
some other hope to give us shape,
  what more of heaven could we ask

than a slow rise to winged song,
dropping darkness like a skin outgrown?

Another Supper

Take this body crinkle-cut
  and deep-fried for us, crisp,
lustrous with oil, steam curling up
  in half-imagined wisps,

for this is even that same seed
  we spread across the dark
red clay, covered six inches deep
  in pitchfork loads of bark,

come back to us a hundred-fold,
  smooth russet-skin and flesh
beyond corruption, baskets full
  of rich, returning life.

Nothing is lost. Whatever falls
  to earth will rise again.
Take it, break, and eat, with salt,
  and ketchup bright as wine.

Reading the Leaves

The sweet gum down the street is scatter-shot
with yellow, sharp-tipped leaves that in the light
wind wink like stars against their rustling night;
our maple turns top first, lets crimson drop
from limb to limb in sunset's daily touch;
and the ash's slow disclosure of itself
spreads evenly, as each leaf like the rest
takes gold that deepens with a faint red blush.
Every tree scrawls its own farewell of flare
and fade—or fade at least. The backyard elm
goes straight to brown. Leaves char, curl on themselves,
and fall, flutter a moment on the air,
show nothing but the ease with which they pass
to settle, scattered on the dying grass.

Last Harvest

A Caterpillar crawls
across the hill, its steel
blade peeling rows
of apple trees. Smoke turns
from gray to black with the strain
of each tree's roots,
then back as they explode
from dirt. By noon, the hill
is striped in lines of grass and bare
red clay. A mix of rotting fruit
and diesel lingers like rain,
sifts down the field to pool
in root-holes, bathe trees piled
like shocks behind the scythe.

Lot

I.

Eyes turned from the bruise of sallow fire
where stone still smoldered down to flakes
the wind could swirl across the plain
or lift to dust their mountain refuge
with the dark and delicate remains
of all they couldn't leave behind,
he crept to her. From higher ground,
the earth looked smooth, a plate of thick,
black glass on which she seemed the last
light left against the spread of darkness.
But this close he could see the perfect
fury of the hand that had shattered
the ground beneath her feet and smeared
the city's dead across her face.

II.

The nights his daughters came to him,
faceless in the play of fire-thrown shadow,
he told himself he didn't know
this flesh so much like hers he had
to rise to it. If he had still
believed in mercy, he'd have prayed
they'd both be barren as the plain
broken beneath its mound of ash.
In his joyless coming he could feel
seeds of destruction great as God
had ever sown, sure as the salt
of her lips lingering on his,
his tongue mixing the residue
of death, the savor of desire.

From Right Field, Looking In

Set on the mound, the fall
                              sun strikes
out batter, fielders,
                              overwrites
the landscape's scrawl
                              with stark, straight lines,
the quick world
                              vanishing behind
a bright
                  simplicity of light,
our radiant
                  and still disguise.
But something
                  of the world abides
there yet. Hidden,
                              a pitcher strides
toward home, a softball's
                              arc invites
a hard reply,
                  and milkweed spikes
the air with seed,
                              the tufted spines
that in their wind-
                              borne drift comprise
the unseen life
                  I hope to find
within the limits
                  of my sight.

Taking the Cake

By twelve the bride and groom
are having their first taste
of wedded—call it bliss,
it could be true—somewhere
beyond these tents emptied
of all but a few servers
stacking plates, balloons
bluntly tumesced, abandoned
chairs and dance floor flattening
the grass—and we, a pack
of poets drunk on more than words,
descend across the green
midnight of moon-washed field
to score two foil-wrapped hunks
of cake, one white, one chocolate,
both taken in hands
back on the dormitory stoop.
Who needs a fork when love
is melting on your tongue, who
wouldn't want to feel the icing,
lick sweet fingers one by one?

Jacob at Peniel

No words, only the shock of what
    his body knows is there,
sudden, unsayable, this weight
    that shudders from the air,

shatters the fabricated light
    his dreaming took for real.
Guiltless and inarticulate,
    the river's long tongue roils

along its banks, mumble of shore
    and swell, the shallow plink
of a rock knocked spinning by a horse,
    bare-backed, coming to drink.

Brought back to earth, he grasps what he
    can grasp, the evidence
beneath his fingertips of sleek
    contours, friction of skin

not unlike his, molding a man
    out of this mystery.
The silver flourish of the moon
    falls soundlessly downstream,

ripples as water laps the mare's shanks,
    mirrors the quick bones
licked by a motion that remains
    when horse and moon are gone.

He wraps his arms around it, digs
    in, holds on as a man
becomes an angel, becomes a God,
    becomes this moment's hand

inside the hollow of his thigh,
    this blur of grief and bliss,
the fervid eloquence that cries
    a name he thinks is his.

A man limps down the riverside
    alone, naked as dawn
subsides to the clear wash of light
    across the yellow stones

beneath his feet, the pool he dives
    into, the liquid spread
his presence makes, the drops that shine
    on his emergent flesh.

II.

Cemetery Orchard: A Ghost Story

No love which this wild rain
Has not dissolved except the love of death,
If love it be for what is perfect and
Cannot, the tempest tells me, disappoint.
     Edward Thomas, "Rain"

no one knows us

now

nameless

lost letters
in this soil

our faces

unlined blossoms pale
in hothouse green
the untranslated streets

our tongues

the rising eloquence
of our decay

stutter and turn to fire

our birth

as living words

a falling scream

pendant
palpable,

already lost

a round-voweled
Done

in a lost world

nothing finishes
death parts for us

out of the treeline

green waves

crested   *always about*
to break   *wash*

us   *our graves*

away

*

Ghosts take root in this clay and bloom,
solid as the tang of windfall apples,
my dead returned as Red Delicious,
Winesap, or these Stayman bending limbs
above your grave as if to hold
you in a green embrace, as if
you might be going anywhere.

Sometimes, I feel you lingering,
echo of jungles on our hills,
a blend of palms and apples, hickory
and betel nuts. The two worlds bleed
together, as firefights keen a high
lament among the trees—mortars,
M-16s, untranslated tongues.

I never see the soldiers, just
bright lines of tracers through the brush.
Mornings, I search the ground for signs:
shell casings, craters, drying blood.
The orchard's as it was, unmarked.
The trees abide, bear heavy fruit
I eat in memory of you.

*

washed into a world
of water
                air heat thick
humid as clouds
                rain and sweat,
rice paddies
                                        ponds we fished as
                                            boys
                rivers,
                                        bream   crappie
                                            small bass
                                        piled on the bank
                                        in glittering sprawls
                the grass rustling
                 unseen
                                        behind us
                dull wet slap
                of flesh
on flesh
                                        on dark clay

*

A photograph of some lost fall.
I'm seven, eight. We're not sure why
we're there, two brothers dressed for war,
our bodies bowed apart, afraid
to touch, our shadows one unending,
blended blur the light compels
across the grass and off the page.

Already you are leaving, weightless
to the wind's unceasing sibilance,
its murmur calling you across
the gray expanse of grass, the scrub
of field pines rising to the hills
and east, past our imaginings.
Already your tongue tests the wind.

*

flesh dark as clay

        gleams
        with sweat

                shaded between
                the rows no breath
                of wind

        streams

as if it comes

                we come

        from water

or is

                we are

        becoming

each splash

                flowing
                into the dust

of bullets
rapid skip across a chest

        already dead

three steps
before   sudden   it knows

*

We filled jars with a light that died
against the glass, and still they came,
endlessly lifting from the grass,
the air so rich each reaching smeared
their brilliant deaths across our hands,
left us a moment luminous
and strange before the shine wore off.

If it wore off. In memory
I see us always in a darkness
seeded with fireflies, filtered stars,
a curl of moon ridge high between
the ground and over-loaded limbs—
the moment's nimbus on our flesh,
the glow of our slow-burning lives.

*

know the sudden
bloom

                             against the darkness

of muzzle flashes

                             appear

                                              cold sparks of light

                             disappear

                                              a kind of dance
                                              with emptiness

                             so strange

cried   not just from fear

                                              a silent music

                             so beautiful

star shells

                                              flicker above
                                              the grass   inside
                                              the weave of limbs
                                              ours   the trees

                             everywhere
                              tongues

of tracers

                             quick

hot

                             whispers
                             almost understood.

*

Caught in the fold-cracked black and white
of your foot-locker photograph,
she turns eternally away,
eyes fixed on where you spill across
her lap in folds of knee and elbow,
waist and neck. Only the cradle
of her hand keeps you from falling.

I don't know who she is, or why
you're there, but you'll rise soon, and pass
beyond embracing, slipping from
this frame where she holds on, and leaning
forward, bathes you in the dark
grace of her hair, still streaming down
to hide you, wash you clean, away.

*

almost understood

        the song a body makes

in barbed wire

             bare to the grasp
             of flesh   the grass
             sliding

snared

        straining
        outlined

             in moonlight

white
phosphorous   screams
fire at the light
a body

        burning

             rising

gives   a clip

             on the flame

        until it stops

*

Your letter when your buddy lost
his right leg at the knee—
                    He liked
            that he could feel it after it
            was gone, the itch he'd scratch in air
            without relief, the throb no drug
            could touch; if it still hurt
            it had to still be part of him.

Such are the strategies we learn
to fill the space where flesh has been,
to turn that incandescent ache
into the light of memory.
My tongue savors the sharpest edge
of your name, craves the dead weight
of a word become unspeakable.

*

never stops

        translating flame

                slow turn season
                to season

        flesh not yet become

a body

                pure speech

a man in fire
clinging   the soul
won't let go   rise

        dull syllables

of bone

                articulation into
                    earth
                hanging   falling

ash   riding air

        away.

*

Your birthday falls among trees stripped
for winter, leaves dead on your grave.
Struck by the spread of limbs too thin
to hold the moon that stutters through
and sets before the sun, I put
on your old glove and throw myself
some flies, lost in the rhythm—pitch,

catch, pitch—till after dark. Each ball
pierces the porch light's shallow dome
as if released by gravity,
and disappears. I wait, my glove
lifted to what my watching calls
out of the night, my only faith
that everything returns to earth.

*

away

                riding the air

                              the rain

we come

                              our names release
                              their letters
                              stones lean   turn
                                        grain
                              by grain

                we go
                the wind

of our own making
lifts us   takes us

                 the green

                              soft earth

returns with us

                always returning

                              the clean wild rain

                 know us now

*

The spring trees burn with blossoms, smear
of flowers, limbs, and leaves, breeze-tossed
across the graves. They let go, bloom
by bloom, petal by petal, smoke
light, soft as ashes. Piled against
tree roots in scented drifts, they melt
to soil. As we do, given time.

When we buried you that June, the still
air flowerless, the lake flat, full
of clouds, reflected trees, I stood
where you taught me the miracle
of walking stones over the whole
inverted world. Side-armed along
the path of rippled light the sun,

setting, cast back across the lake,
a stone could skip a dozen times
before it sank, or vanished in
the glare. We couldn't tell. And I
can't now. Each step puts everything
in play, reshapes the lake, the sky,
the trees, the two of us who watched,

washed in the change ourselves,
our image shimmering and strange
until the water calmed enough
for us to see what we'd become.
And in our trembling we remained
the slow voice of the world, the tongue
we spoke, the tongue that speaks us still.

III.

Driving Home

Fear drives men to faith—Martin Luther

I-40 vanishes in fog so thick
it slaps my high-beams back like sinners' prayers,
without effect even if something's there.
There may be nothing but this slow, gray drift
into the half-imagined world I strain
to see: a few bare feet of pot-holed road,
tinted by the weak, admonitory glow,
dull red, of highway markers glazed with rain.
I pray from fear, when my father hacks the waste
of something fierce and feeding in his chest,
or when my mother can't recall my name,
or when, tonight, I'm hours away, it's late,
our phone rings unrelieved, and you're not home.
I crawl through darkness, pray you wait in light.

"This Is the Best Christmas Ever"

The drama was all but done, the sort
        our country Baptist church
put on each year—an orphanage
        of kids bereft of hope,

belief, or anything except
        the cold some banker's just
about to throw them trembling out
        into. But then, on cue,

a Christmas miracle, complete
        with the old tale retold
as with two orphans on his knees,
        some borrowed father reads

the shepherds down the aisle to where
        the plastic Christ-child lies.
Hard hearts are changed, the orphanage
        is saved, and the youngest there,

the one who'd been the worst, who'd reveled
        in his lack of faith, can stand
transformed, his face spotlit to burn
        with God's sweet fire, his tongue

rich with the final line, to bring
        the curtain down and lift
the shadowed crowd, the words the angels
        in the wings, the wise men knelt

near father, mother, child wait for.
        And almost through, he vomits,
and runs, as we run from prophecy
        when we can see its truth.

Preacher in Fall

—for Pat F.

Eli, Eli, lama sabacthani.

My trees are bare, the back yard bruised
      Yellow-brown. Maple streaks
Glint wetly crimson where the bursts
      Of headlights from the street
Dispense staccato revelation,
      Whatever afternoon's
Half-light had camouflaged as sameness
      Yanked briefly into view.

Heaven might lie in clarity,
      A sudden apprehension,
Subtle and sinuous—red leaves
      Tracing a pattern on
The grass, this morning's flight of crows
      Holding the ragged time
Of my heart watching them compose
      Unreachable design

From the random gather and release
      Of birds on wing, the sky
Returned to utter vacancy,
      Stoic and stupefied,
After they pass. And watching, I
      Know only that the night
Erases all of this, desires
      Nothing, its long ascent

Moving without regard for us,
      Enormous and alone.

On Beauty

Forget that we were sixteen, seventeen,
  and ignorant, that all we knew of art
were Tolkien calendars and the air-brushed sheen
  of paper nipples, lips, thighs split apart;

forget we'd spent the evening slamming back
  sixteen-ounce stovepipe cans of bootlegged Strohs,
and smoking homegrown pot so harsh it hacked
  networks of fleshy canyons down our throats;

instead remember this: how at night's close,
after we'd put the propane out, we rose

into the smeared and lingering trail of light
the evening's final cigarette described

against the slate the lantern left because
it was beautiful, and we knew it was.

Eureka Springs

I could get used to this—
the anniversary champagne,
         our spill from heart-shaped tub
            to love, to sleep,

        then coffee on the porch,
watching what I suppose must be,
        morning by morning, the same
           rabbit cropping

        grass where our yard fades
to brush, even the daily grace
        of buzzards gliding to roost—
           quick, blameless

        silhouettes breaking
the sunrise frame of sycamore
        and water oak that casts
            our view as a triptych

        of shorelines, banks of mist
above three surely seamless rivers.
        Whatever Heraclitus
           might have said

        of time, its taloned flow,
of wings that carry us without
        a hope of standing still
           or turning back,

        today will have the heft
of yesterday, the Ozarks' August
        heat draped over us,
           our walk pine-scented,

dimmed, a breath across
the water's face, and buzzards circling.
My love, turn out the light.
Come back to bed.

Storm Light

A deeper shade seeps through
the night, snuffs stars out one
by one. The storm is stunning,
its violence beautiful
as lightning shreds the sky,
our bedroom dark and light
in turn. Each flare unveils
my wife, then slips a fold
of darkness over her.

Seen in this fitful light,
her face is empty, calm.
But I have learned to keep
a weather eye. I love
my wife, if love can have
so much of need, and she
loves me, if storms can love
the trees bent to their wind,
the ground beneath their rain.

Penelope Redecorates

The couch, shuttled from wall to wall and back,
>   or to the middle of the floor,
faces now the TV, now flames picking
>   out red and gold threads from the weave,
as rooms spin into place—the mismatched end
>   tables there, brass floor lamps flanking
his leather chair, the ottoman rolled just
>   in front. Her art lies in the pain
she takes, arranging photographs to frame
>   a tale of bliss, wedding silver
candlesticks to yard-sale bric-a-brac,
>   finding the right spot for *Tournee*
du Chat Noir. On the long commute from Memphis,
>   he never knows what living room
he'll find, or where the bed will be, but knows
>   each space ephemeral as the one
before, the one she'll make again by dawn,
>   since stopping means a life reduced
to rooms that never fit, a stranger coming
>   through what was the bedroom door.

Leaving the Garden

I. Salad Days

Runners of green and butter beans bound up
in twine, she lifts her t-shirt—quick, brown flash
of belly's curve, bright beads of sweat—and rubs
a Better Boy until it gleams, red, lush,
ready to open at the lightest touch
of teeth. She bites deep, and offers him
a taste, the appetite of flesh for flesh
as liquid as the juice across her lips,
as certain as the cloudless August sky.
They stumble through the garden shedding clothes
and tangled vines, shuck down to sun-ripe skin
piquant with the salt they earn their pleasure in,
an ooze of oil on brows, backs, breasts, on thighs
stippled with the light falling through their rows.

II. Fall Party

She picks up socks and books, a fast-
        food bag from lunch, while he removes
        the fall of twigs and half-turned leaves
a storm had dropped across the grass,

the litter of their days. By night,
        their rooms will gleam like store displays,
        back yard a temporary blaze
of candlesticks and Christmas lights,

but now she scrubs the sink, he sweeps
        the patio, pulls up the roots
of thyme and basil they won't eat,

        a Roma vine loaded the summer through
still heavy with the sweet increase
        they've neither touched, nor wanted to.

III. Eclipse

His circuit through the dark
   from patio to potting-shed
evokes a sensual mirage

of summer heat and white-pine bark.
   Fistfuls of mulch they'd spread
in May have frozen hard

around the clumps of Cupid's Dart,
   Beebalm, and Baby's Breath.
Watching, she knows his arc

as absences: a porch light swept
   by emptiness, the blur
of shadow on the bright prospect

the TV next door holds, the hush
of wind-chimes silenced by his touch.

IV. Perennials

Bright gasps of daffodils already come
and passed from the untended beds, thick clumps

of blunt-tipped, pale green shafts too tall to bear
unbent the fading drive of their own weight

relax, sag back among the tulips' spent
luxuriance of petals fallen past

the horizontal. Irises, untouched
by human hands, open their fine-haired buds,

and soon the season's easy stroke will coax
pink peonies, delphinium, and phlox

to spread themselves to sunlight's sweep across
the sidewalk flower plots, the uncut grass

spotted again with dandelions, and now,
the realtor's sign before the empty house.

The Fall Apart

I want to tell her how it is
        here, that the leaves fall through
the palette they have always used,
        that each night stays

a little longer than the last
        before a colder blue
dawns on the stagnant avenues,
        that light still slips

down its accustomed path to her
        side of the bed, the air
        embodied as the stir

of random, lifeless bits of skin
        lost in the wind
        she left behind.

Making Beds

Cradle of knotty pine,
        hand-planed to outlast need,
        hold a son's son in sleep;
the marriage bed half done,

keeping its wait in vain;
        now this. His buzzsaw screams
        through oak, the thick scent sweet
and rising, the dust in fine

descent on everything—
        his shirt's rough weave, his face,
        his hands brushing the cuts,
hard fingers lingering
        on the grain before they set
        each stolid board in place.

Child of Age

My grandma is a girl again,
and I'm her father when I visit
on Sunday afternoons. She sits
straight-backed, prim in the faultless white
returned to her by years that wipe
her memory clean of children
and the kiss of loved skin burning hers.
She doesn't know sweat, or passion
in this pallid world she calls her school.
We talk of friends and playmates dead
before my birth until I seem
to see them, hear their high-pitched shouts.
She waves her hands in speech, or hides
them in a clever fold of cloth
to keep their ragged, bitten nails
from me. I bring her cookies
but I think her body only needs
itself to feed on now. She gets
smaller each time I see her. Soon,
she'll be an egg, and then a notion.

My Grandfather Waits for Sleep

The body wants what it can't name
beyond this vague space his hands shape,

no hint of mind in their slow weave
along the muscles' memory,

long labor rutted in the bone.
His saw-lopped fingers can't let go

of what still slips their grasp, shuck corn
or rip rough poplar, board by board.

Or something else, an emptiness
that fades and recollects itself,

hanging between them as they rise
and fall, the figure of desire

leading to this: a latch he strains
to lift, doorknob he almost turns.

For the Dead One

October, and the rain falls through
        a crown of oak, falls to

the dogwood's dark leaves, falls on stumps
        still oozing sap, on laps

left where they dropped, on mounds of dust
        saw-spit at every cut,

falls in the ruts of tractor tires.
        No one among the trees,

or in the log yard, only rain,
        red clay, a plastic ring

of buckets upside down, charred ends
        of branches, soft-drink cans,

scatter of wrappers, paper bags,
        a barrel full of ash.

Seed Time

The front yard surges into spring,
grass greens and thickens, the Bradford pear
flickers quickly white, then its pale
        summer shade begins

again, the same as every year,
clear, yellow light swelling the days,
all absolutely commonplace.
        And not like this before.

If a tree falls in the woods, and no
one's there, is it still beautiful—
wind rising through that dying fall,
        leaves singing though they go

unheard? What use is beauty left
uncomprehended, pitched past our
perception, a call too high to hear,
        an elegance unfelt?

What good is an unravished flower?
The yard compels us to its quick,
relentless pace, the vivid whips
        forsythia unfurls

against the deck, redbuds so fierce
in their unthinking urge to bloom
they won't be limited to limbs,
        stream down the trunks, bright smears

of lavender along the bark,
life pushing always out of bounds.
The dogwood soon will bare their crowns
        of thorns beside the barn

and far across the empty fields,
white wisps half seen beneath the lush
burden of uncurled leaves that ash,
        sweet gum, and poplar lift.

For years, no hickory could lean
without his weight against the trunk,
no stand of pine or chestnut oak
        could fall without his hand

to grip the chainsaw's throttle, guide
its whine and grumble through the rough,
ringed histories that, rain or drought,
        finally subside alike

to the flat reflection of a touch
across a table's polished grain,
wood recollected more as the fragrance
        of fine, sharp-scented dust

than as the thing itself. The mind,
caught by the gravity of flesh,
falls inward as the body fails,
        a trajectory described

in ever-shrinking arcs, a world
reduced to the contours of a couch,
a bed, the intervening stretch
        of shuffled hardwood floor.

The shed's stained, sagging doors stay closed
on bags of nitrogen and lime,
seed-spreaders, saws, a cobwebbed file
        of axes, spades and hoes.

Of course, the densely petalled dome
of the Yoshimo cherry tree
is beautiful alone, as are
      the bees, their luscious hum

among the blooms, but all that grows
out of the garden's unturned earth
are beggar-lice and cockle-burs,
      wild grasses where the rows

of corn and twine-bound beans have been.
There is no sense in this, no way
to make sense of what time makes
      of us. Nothing beyond

his window waits for him to bring
it into being, nothing inside
him now requires his will to speed
      its soon and certain rising.

If he still sees it so, a kind
of blossoming in which he'll break
at last, a bud blown for the taking.
      Does he believe a wind

will lift him up, a rush of wings
will gather something wholly him,
a seed to rise another time,
      come some celestial spring?

I can't imagine any life
but this, rooted in common soil,
the ground of our uneasy loves,
      imperfect, restless, brief,

and still impossibly sweet.
Nothing is certain, nothing calls
with clarity and heft. This could
            be beautiful, could be

all we've been wanting for so long:
a meadow, silent, dark with shade
from unseen trees, our very names
            forgotten on our tongues.

Biography

Born and reared in Taylorsville, in the foothills of North Carolina, Bob Watts teaches at Lehigh University in Bethlehem, PA, along with his wife, the writer Stephanie Powell Watts. His poems have appeared in *Poetry, The Paris Review,* and *Southern Poetry Review*, among other journals. One of the founding co-editors of *Center: A Journal of the Literary Arts*, he holds the Creative Writing PhD in English from the University of Missouri-Columbia.

10/13

Albert Carlton - Cashiers
Community Library
PO Box 2127

9 781932 339765